the *place* making factor:

[a catalyst for disrupting environment and social grant making]

maria adebowale-schwarte

living space project

The Place Making Factor – A catalyst for disrupting environment and social funding

living space project

First published in 2016 by Living Space Project
www.livingspaceproject.com
www.theplacemakingfactor.com

Book cover design by Jenny Owen
Book design by Neil Coe, Carta Design
Book edited by Lorna Howarth, The Write Factor

Printed on paper from responsible sources

ISBN: 0-9547255-3-0

A CIP catalogue record for this book is available from the British Library.

Supported by:

Clore Social Leadership

Esmée Fairbairn Foundation

To find out more about placemaking, research, projects, training and other publication visit www.livingspaceproject.com

about

living space project

Living Space Project is an urban placemaking and green space consultancy and think tank. It operates as a social enterprise and, is dedicated to connecting people through urban places and green spaces. Its values are based on the belief that everyone should be able to enjoy a good place to live, love, work and play. Because good places, and green spaces, create better lives.

Living Space Project focuses on creating successful places in diverse urban neighbourhoods and cities, dedicated to equality, collaboration and fascinated by people and placemaking. And has decades of experience delivering research and practical projects.

It believes that transforming cities and neighbourhoods through placemaking rejuvenates not only spaces but drives local economies, and connects people - project by project, city by city, neighbourhood by neighbourhood, community by community.

For Living Space Project good placemaking always comes about through conversations, relationship building, action and learning. That's why it focuses on collective and collaborative placemaking.

Its work is local, national and international. Supporting communities, architects, developers, local authorities, charitable foundations, central government, academics and international agencies on built and green spaces.

Living Space Project's clients gain crucial advice, research, and ideas for developing place making briefs, plans, projects and policy.

www.livingspaceproject.com/about-us/

clore social leadership fellowship programme

The Fellowship is a multi-faceted, holistic approach to developing people which includes coaching, residentials, and action learning.

Every year social leaders from across the UK apply to become one of the Clore Social Fellows. After a competitive application process, we select around 20 of them to become part of our next cohort of social leaders.

It constantly strives for excellence and to be responsive to the changing needs of the sector. Each year we review our programme and make changes and improvements, so the shape of the programme changes with every cohort.

The short answer to why the Fellowship is so important is because people are the ones who create social change. Developing effective, resilient leaders will make for stronger, better led organisations, and leadership that transforms lives. It underpins everything we do.

www.cloresocialleadership.org.uk/Fellowship-Programme

esmée fairbairn foundation

The Esmée Fairbairn Foundation aims to improve the quality of life for people and communities throughout the UK, both now and in the future. They do this by funding the charitable work of organisations with the ideas and ability to achieve positive change.

The Foundation is one of the largest independent grant makers in the UK. They make grants in the region of £35 million annually towards a wide range of work within the arts, children and young people, the environment and social change. They also make up to £35 million in social investments in organisations that aim to deliver both a financial return and a social benefit.

Across all their funding they aim to unlock and enable potential, back the unorthodox and unfashionable, build collective networks and catalyse system change.

They offer three types of support: grants, social investments and grants plus support.

www.esmeefairbairn.org.uk/who-we-are/

contents

1.

an introduction - why places matters

In the summer of the mid-90's, I saw an advert in The Guardian for a job at an environmental non- governmental organisation. It was to be the beginning of my relationship with the environmental sector for which I have a deep respect and concern for.

Here was a sector that with all its heart was trying to protect the planet. It was made up of people deeply committed to the cause. But, here's also was a sector that struggled to understand that its objective was about environment and people, and not just about 'educating the public to understand the environment' – but rather, fitting the environment around people and the places they live.

This short book is influenced by twenty years' experience of working in the environmental sector, specifically inclusion and placemaking, and with one of the biggest and most influential groups in the social sector: charitable foundations and grant makers. But, it's also a project that's heavily informed by almost eighteen months of research as the first recipient of the Environment Clore Fellowship.

Being the first Environment Fellow has been a pretty privileged position. It's not often you get real time to reflect. I've had a free reign to talk about, debate, question and learn from environmentalists, developers, activists, planners, funders, urban designers, and communities in struggling neighbourhoods from diverse diasporas and backgrounds.

The Place Making Factor is a reflection on a simple idea. And it's this: what is crucial for the environmental and social sector, is that they don't lose sight of three facts. First, people's intrinsic connections to local place inform how they feel about the environment at a local level. Second, place is an incredibly powerful convergence tool for social, and economic change. And third, grant makers can use placemaking to disrupt old patterns of siloed grant funding.

Factoring 'place' into the story of the environment and social change is a powerful hook for people who do not consider themselves to be environmentalists, yet care about the environment – and of course, for people who consider themselves environmentalists and care about people. The ability to understand the environment and people through the social and economic lens of streets, neighbourhoods and cities brings our thinking into the real world about the environment sector and gets buy-in from people who feel ostracised from the environment agenda and what they think it stands for.

The thing is, the environment – in particular for people living in struggling neighbourhoods – is what we see when our curtains get opened, and we look out of the window: the grey and green space that is outside. And that's something the environment and social sector all too often overlook.

Of course, conservation and climate change are part of the big environmental agenda. And, a 'deep green' understanding of the environment is helpful. The environment must be protected and conserved for its intrinsic value. But this shouldn't negate the fact that the environment is an economic asset, offering social capital and relational ties for making better places. Which is one of the biggest reasons why placemaking must be part of a grant making agenda that's wider than it currently is.

The rest of this book looks at what placemaking is and what it means for grant making. It includes a series of interviews and 'off the record' conversations with environment grant makers and placemakers in London, New York, Stockholm and Rotterdam, who are effective partners in delivering better prospects for urban renewal, environment and green spaces. I've used quotes from these conversations, highlighted in orange, throughout.

It offers a focus on the grant funding experience of dealing with multiple threats to the environment as well as tackling social justice in a complex, ever-urbanising and diverse society. Ultimately, that means grant making and funding of environmental projects has to adapt strategically to provide grant investment driven by place and placemaking.

2. reconciling perspectives: environment and place

the *place* making factor:

Pocket Park
New York: Earth People

environment – where we're at

"There should be no one story to the environment, it has intersections between urban, rural, water, justice and health."[1]

perceptions:

What is the 'environment sector' and what is its focus? When I've asked this question to the hundreds of communities I've worked with, the response is generally along the lines of:

big environmental charities only care about nature not people.

they're interested in the countryside and stuff like that, not where we live.

it's a bit white and middle class.

These are contested perspectives, for example, caring about the environment, is neither a white, middle class, rural or urban agenda. But the above heartfelt views have been expressed by people who care about the environment but do not see themselves as environmentalists. Every one of these comments has come from folk deeply involved in improving their local environment via green spaces, food growing, health and wellbeing, and land management training and jobs.

1 All quotes highlighted in orange are taken from 'off the record' conversations with grant makers, and placemakers based in London, New York, Stockholm and Rotterdam.

They talk passionately about creating better places to live in and consequently, better lives for their families and neighbours. The focus is on making places better – streets, neighbourhoods or even small patches of ground – and of course, the environment is an essential part of that. Turning these places around is about using the environment and green spaces in the context of a package of local assets for jobs, inclusion and wellbeing.

perceptions of place

Perhaps the best way to start understanding the placemaking factor is by looking at people's perceptions of place. Our first impressions start with the intangible connections to physical space: the green and grey spaces we use, in and around buildings.

It begins with the feeling a place provides: the images we have based on sight, sounds and smell, and the activities and meaning we collectively or individually give to the local pocket park, the abandoned front gardens, high streets, the stream in the woods or the local playground. Place is an intangible morphology of what we love or hate about where we live, play or visit.

What's personal to us helps to make sense of the emotions and connections we feel about the bricks and trees that make up our urban environment. They create either a feeling of belonging to a place, of pride about it or anger, fear, dislike or a desire to leave.

sense of place

A Sense of Place, Diagram 1 (Image adapted Tim Heath,Professor Taner Oc, and Steve Tiesdell)

How we 'sense' a place is particular to one person or community. Our view of a place can be partial or distorted, but also real. We may subconsciously discriminate against a place when a park is run down, and there is more dog shit and litter than flowers or swings. Similarly, we may notice that trees line the streets in the posh part of town, but weeds in the not so posh part.

Place defines who we are as individuals and as a society. Places shape who we are or what we want, as much our social networks and political beliefs. And the places we provide for people to live in are a measure of how much we respect human rights, fair economics and the environment. It's perhaps not surprising that the United Nation Human Settlements Programme, better known as UN Habitat, promoted the Year of Placemaking in 2015, and launched the Global Public Space Programme four years earlier. The UN Sustainable Development Goals, aimed at transforming the world and to which the UK is signed up to, includes Goal 11. It's purpose:

"to make cities inclusive, safe, resilient and sustainable"
UN, Sustainable Development Goal 11

A strong part of this agenda, is placemaking and the ability to leverage its impacts for rural, and urban living.

What a city looks and feels like at neighbourhood and street level is a significant factor for investment in the area, the people and business. And the health and resilience of a city is massively defined by its physical setting, the activities that happen there and the quality of a place.

"Whatever space and time mean, place and occasion mean more."
Aldo Van Eyck

connected history and politics

One of the easiest ways of understanding the connection to environment and place is from their comparative agendas and history. Environment and place are two concepts that are historically connected, with deep affiliations to social justice.

"The environment is a connector – it's people orientated, and connected to better places and cities for people"

history

Historically, protecting the environment has always been surrounded by tensions of meaning, perspective and political dogma. It's a false binary debate – you're either a committed 'deep green' environmentalist or a 'light green', or you simply don't care about the environment and therefore, will go to hell in a hand cart. The deep green's dogma is that the environment is valuable for its own sake, without any connection to the wellbeing of people. The light greens challenge this non -anthropocentric view. For them, the environment can only be understood through people 's connection to it. Its principal value lies in the fact that our survival and wellbeing is dependent on it.

Both schools of thought are right, but it's pretty difficult – some would say naïve – to see the value of the environment as divorced from its connection to people and places.

How we have protected the environment, through regulation, policy and protest has more often than not been connected to the need for conservation, and access to public assets such as forests, water, wilderness and land for habitation.

In England, the development of environmental regulation went hand in hand with regulation for the much-needed improvement of public health and alleviation of poverty.

Protecting the environment, town planning, housing and the provision of public playgrounds and parks, is part of a national psyche to protect people, place and the environment. And it's deeply connected to the belief that there needs to be a 'level playing field'.

The problem is, the level playing field proves to be crucial yet continuously elusive.

When academics Erik Swyngedouw and Nikolas C. Heynen commented on place and environment in their article on Urban Political Ecology, they noted that urban place is an

> *"unexplored phenomenon in the relationships between environmental injustice and … urbanisation processes"*

They recognised that urban ecology has its roots in industrialisation and the consequent internal and external environmental improvements that benefited cities and homes. Swyngedouw and Heynen go on to reflect that the connectedness to urban place is a useful way to explore social and environmental changes.

What's strikes me is how the authors' views so firmly articulate the conversations I've had in the last eighteen months with communities living with poverty and the organisations working with them. I recognise the deep connection to place that people speak of, and the deep concerns they have for the environment and economic inequality, which Swyngedouw and Heynen, referred to as:

"ecological war zones of depressed neighbourhoods"

The politics of place, environment, equity and urbanism are intrinsically linked. Neighbourhoods continue to express the feeling of exclusion from the traditional environmental movement. The y feel their presence is invisible, and relates to issues of race, class and low income, which are a 'no show' in environmental campaigns and also, in grant programmes available for nuanced urban environment and socially relevant placemaking projects.

Understanding the environment and how environmental projects are funded requires constant focus on one question: who and what does the project benefit? And, in an increasingly urbanised world, answering this question requires understanding the speed at which the environment and nature bec ome urbanised and interact with people's daily lives.

Cities, neighbourhoods and place then, are part and parcel of an integrated urban process. For that reason, they are a strategic starting point for protecting the environment and tackling social and economic benefits without a siloed approach.

Jane Jacobs, perhaps one of the most famous commentators on cities and urban places, noted in a delightfully picturesque way cities and urban place are:

> *"as natural as colonies of prairie dogs or the beds of oysters".*

Nature and human settlements are inextricably linked. Ignoring or not paying enough attention to the role of placemaking in the environment and social sectors creates an uneven distribution and impact of environmental and economic goods and bads.

3. place: collaboration and convergence

the *place* making factor:

Collective use of space between buildings, New York

place: as a convergence model

The successful development of grant funding for environmental and social projects depends heavily on just how it deals with place and inclusion. Fundamentally, it's about creating a monumental shift in the culture and the political standpoint of the grant makers to placemaking and place.

Traditionally, the environmental movement in England and to some extent in the United States has dealt with environmental degradation by encouraging conservation, penalising polluters and attempting to change the public behaviour. The people most affected by the consequences of environmental decision making are not only alienated from a narrow debate and insufficiently protected by environmental or economic policy but have felt let down by grant making.

For this to change we need to get some clarity on the use of place as a convergence tool – because placemaking can not only protect the local environment but also lever economic and social capital for the people that need it most.

green spaces, place and placemaking

Over the last twenty years, I've never met a person or a community group that hasn't connected to theenvironment through green spaces in their neighbourhood, street or town.

green space

If you Google the definition of 'green spaces' you will probably find the following:

> *"green space (noun)*
>
> *an area of grass, trees or other vegetation set apart for recreational or aesthetic purposes in an otherwise urban area."*

But in the real world, community groups see green space as having a far wider meaning. It's defined as:

> *'green space (noun)*
>
> *parks, trees, forests, public-facing gardens, playing fields, cemeteries, green corridors, allotments, spaces between buildings, play areas, woods, rivers, streams, beaches, canals, hanging baskets on local high streets, raised beds, and tree bases.'*

place

Good public places whether grey or green are underlying assets for urban renewal, wellbeing, and developing local economies that provide jobs and training. Place, in essence, is the sweet spot that connects the environment to green spaces to social inclusion and fair economics. It creates stakeholders with a strong sense of responsibility to the local (and arguably global) environment.

It's not only about the intangible sense of place but about the tangible environmental benefits required for urban living where people thrive.

Put simply, placemaking gives environment an identity that people from vastly diverse backgrounds feel connected to. And placemaking is the participative process that creates good places for a better environment and healthier lives. The longer explanation is that placemaking is a 'multi-faceted' process around private/public spaces: grey (built) and green (natural) space ownership, governance, planning, design and management of public places. The primary placemaking principle is that cities and urban neighbourhoods are created and developed to maximise shared values, assets and wellbeing through a participatory bottom-up process convergence.

"Place is an open book it can be a thousand things. It allows for thinking with broader dimensions. It's about attachment, emotional, connection, engagement and empowerment...and ownership."

I visited Fred and Ethan Kent, of Project for Public Spaces (PPS), a founding placemaking organisation, in downtown East Village, New York. We sat at a large table in their office with other members of PPS team and had a lively conversation about our views on placemaking as a convergence factor. We disagreed on some things but agreed on most. They also see placemaking as a driver for environmental issues and urban and community development. It provides narrative and process for a robust framework for community collaboration to their physical habitat.

Taking on board the discussion with Ethan and Fred, I think that there are two levels of convergence that centre around placemaking: the primary and the secondary level.

The primary level connections are local food systems, public health, climate change resilience, green jobs and economy, environmental stewardship, access to environmental decision-making, and green space equity.

The secondary level focuses on wider political movements or disciplines of city -wide renewal, smart growth, transportation, green buildings, public ownership of green space, architectural design, town planning and land use.

Placemaking: a convergence model, diagram 2.

Both secondary and primary levels of convergence are closely linked to the environment, society and economy. Each level reflects just how placemaking can act as a catalyst for change.

Running through the three convergence areas are six social activation points. I call them the REDPINS:

- Relationships – creating relational ties and networks
- Equitable environments – equal access to environmental goods
- Design – by and with communities to meet social and environmental human needs
- Public Realm – stays at the heart of a neighbourhood and is not lost to private ownership
- Inclusive - open to everyone and not limited to the few
- Neighbourly - neighbourhoods that feel connected, safe and inclusive
- Safety – tackling crime and fear of crime by welcoming all communities back into public spaces

The REDPINS shine spotlights on people's roles in placemaking. As Richard Rogers, architect and commentator on placemaking said, place = people + communities.

I think the REDPINS act as springboards for, "restoring humanity's harmony with nature", something Rogers stated was at the heart for a small planet living.

You can see how the activation points are used or are present in the following place stories.

4. place stories

Festival of Neighbourhood, Southbank, London

Detroit: food growing, urban farming and renewal advocacy

Detroit is a city of scale, made rich by industry, and broken by the banks. It's a much used example of the economic crisis, urban flight and makes the case for urban renewal.

But now, Detroit is moving from a city based on the motor vehicle to a city reshaping itself through the placemaking vehicle. When I visited Detroit, I spent time visiting neighbourhoods and the city's quarters and green space projects. Poverty here has hit hard, it is palpable; it's left few areas, homes and people untouched.

Growing food is one answer to poverty and the need for reskilling. And, throughout Detroit, almost on every other block, are effective spaces dedicated to growing food and flowers – from the size of a wooden fruit crate to backyard gardens.

A few blocks down from some of the hipster coffee shops, I found spaces were people could not only grow their own food but take produce for free from boxes left outside the entrance.

Walking through the streets lined with skyscrapers, derelict buildings and pocket parks, I found Lafayette Greens, part of Greening Detroit Project, a programme to green the city, create jobs and grow food. Lafayette Green is small space of land between high-rise buildings next to a hotel car park. It is a beautifully cared for space displaying a colourful variety of vegetables and plants. To the side is a red brick wall with an entrance to a café and seats where anyone – resident or worker – can sit and feel the stillness, away from the hectic metropolis.

Lafayette Green, Detroit

But, the best part of Lafayette Green was talking to four wonderful women, between the ages of 70 and 85 years of age. This place is important to them – it provides healthy food crucial for a stretched budget, plus the kindling of new and old friendships. And, both of these are reasons why one of the women, aged 80, gets up at six o'clock in the morning to make the one hour walk to the Green from her home. As we spoke, they were consistent in their 'A' rate review, not only of the space itself but because it's used as a place to train green job apprenticeships on land management and food growing for the younger generation.

Continuing on this Detroit walk, I also found the City Beach. Funded by the Kresge Foundation, it was an example of another way the city is using space as a tool for inclusive renewal.

Here families, and friends reflecting a diversity of ethnicity and age – talk, drink and play. If you have money you can buy a drink from the mobile bar, but if you don't you can just bring your food and drink. It's a bit of a textbook example a great place – welcoming, sociable, diverse, and charming. It's close to some of the major restaurants and retail shops so it has the potential to press the 'developing the local economy' button too.

Also based in Detroit is CDAD, the Community Development Advocates of Detroit. CDAD sees its role as a catalyst for the renewal and transformation of neighbourhoods in the city. It tackles urban flight from Detroit, poverty, values, and the challenges of people and place and CDAD runs a neighbourhood placemaking programme. The CDAD programme – also supported by the Kresge Foundation – provides small grants to placemaking projects. They do this as a way to use public spaces to bring people to together as part of a much-needed urban renewal of neighbourhoods – that in their words, "that develops strong community engagement" and tackle access and safety concerns.

It's a work in progress but with grantees of the $42,000 programme creating places such as peace zones, and arts and culture pocket parks designed with rehab and fitness in mind, it's small scale but crucially uses placemaking as a tool to keep neighbourhoods vibrant and strong.

Rotterdam: long term ownership, co-creation and resilience

What makes Rotterdam a leader in placemaking is the way the city is always seeking to improve its 'liveability' by tactical use of building, space and street design. This city has a deep belief in renewal and that transitioning happens when all are equal stakeholders. Here, agencies, individuals, community groups, and municipalities are equal partners in transforming the city in a way that works.

In a transformed railway arch a spit away from Hopflein Station, at the end of a short walk over a yellow pedestrian bridge, I sat in the ICLEI Informed Cities conference listening to stories about placemaking projects happening in Rotterdam and the Netherlands.

Here I heard about the placemaking agenda being fundamental to a city 's master plan for economic, environmental and social transition. At the heart of this liveability program is the investment in innovative community and collaborative projects. "Rotterdam people make the city," was how one of the speakers expressed it. The city invested time in projects like ICLEI, to understand how Rotterdam can co-create a city of tomorrow. One crucial part of this is for local government to take care of the common interests of all.

Creating this future requires deep investment, and they see their reference point as the international human right to 'resilient public places and spaces for all'. For that reason, the city, with crucial grants and support from the Rockefeller

Foundation's pioneering Top 100 Resilient Cities programme, is deep-diving into placemaking as a tool for city-wide resilience.

This deep dive into placemaking requires a lifelong commitment. There is no 'sell by' date attached.

Big Local Northfleet and No Wall Gardens: training, jobs and enterprise

When the Living Space Project joined the Local Trust Delivery Partnership to run the Big Local Environment & Place programme, one of the first things it did was to set up a pilot project hub.

Run over two years by Living Space Project, the placemaking 'think and do' tank, we worked with a number of Big Local areas, who had applied to be pilot hubs. What struck me almost immediately, was how deeply connected green spaces and local environment are rooted in a community's sense of place.

Our first pilot project, Big Local Northfleet, is based in the south-east of England, at the edge of Gravesend and Dartford. It took me thirty minutes to get there by train, which trundled past luxury brand shopping outlets, houses, industrial buildings and a strikingly green corridor of fields and marshland.

Northfleet is one of the Big Local areas awarded one million pounds by Big Local (a project run by the Local Trust) for communities to make their areas 'even better places to live' over ten years.

At my first meeting with Big Local Northfleet, I was impressed by the enthusiasm in the room. The meeting held at a local community centre included local councillors, a major supermarket, the local police, historians, and budding social entrepreneurs, as well as interested community members.

Carl Adams, a Big Local Rep supporting the area at that time, put it best when he said that, "for Big Local Northfleet, the reason why people got involved was not about the money but about creating a great place to live."

For them, 'great place' included valuing its local heritage and green spaces. The group felt it needed to be made more accessible, loved again and used to develop social enterprises that provided jobs and training for people living in the area.

No Walls Gardens is one such social enterprise. Set up as a Community Interest Company, it uses garden and green space projects as a tool for placemaking in Northfleet, providing gardening and landscape skills to volunteers, including people often excluded from traditional job markets, including people recovering from addiction or who are a long-term unemployed.

You can watch the No Walls Garden, People, Place and Environment video, on the Living Space Project website. If you do you'll see their absolute enthusiasm for what they do, and why they do it. And, if you meet them face to face you'll be hit by an enormous 'can do' attitude, matched with plans of actions, and grants and partnerships coming from the European Union to the famous Eden Project.

It's possible that Gardens Without Walls may have started without Big Local Trust's grant to Northfleet, but it's clear that Big Local's presence, offering advice and financial support, is a catalyst for placemaking ideas that create social enterprises and economic assets.

596 acres: access to land advocacy and data collation tools

I met 596 Acres on an incredibly hot day in Brooklyn, New York. I walked under the railway tracks, past rows of houses and local shops, regretting wearing a top with more polyester than is required for human comfort.

I eventually identified the plot where I agreed to meet 596, by the semi-circle of people who were sitting talking in a well-loved fenced-off garden. Paula, the Founding Director of 596 Acres, sees me and waves. I'm at the right place. I sit and listen to the people at the meeting. Two community members, a part-time high school teacher and a retired truck driver are speaking. He explains later that he got involved with 596 Acres because he wanted to be a gardener, all his life and 596 offered just the support he was looking for to find a plot.

The group talk about their plots and the gardening; the teacher mentions that's she sells her surplus produce at local food markets, but that sometimes people don't want to spend their money on good quality food, or just simply don't have a clue how to cook vegetables they don't recognise. A third woman joins later, and she mentions that she needs more administrative help to get hold of a plot like the one where sitting in. A member of the 596 team offers to help her, the woman thanks her, and takes up the offer mentioning that her daughter had said she would help, but just hasn't found the time.

All three of the people sitting in this urban garden are here on a hot day because 596 understand how to utilise the data necessary to get access to land – it is a powerful advocacy tool. They've helped hundreds more since they started, all around New York , and in other countries too – sharing data, providing community support and campaigning for access to land.

In their words, 596 are dedicated to, 'creating a practice of building online tools that neighbours can use to remove the hurdles to community land access. These tools turn city data into information about particular pieces of land and connect people to one another through simple social networking functions'. They also support groups to create land access tools in NY and other cities via their open source code and practical mentorships.

When I get introduced to the group, I have a discussion with Paula about how gaining access to a plot is a catalyst for getting involved with wider decision-making issues around neighbourhood placemaking.

Data that maps land and space, and its ownership, is critical. But, it strikes me that the difficulty is not only in finding land, but owning the land. In my experience, communities in England despite, access to land registries, are consistently worn down – not only by finding land, but also finding out who owns it. I've heard from far too many communities and individuals about having to spend unwaged time of eighteen months and longer, to get through a series of wild goose chases to try and find land owners.

The location of some landowners are discovered in a matter of days, and they're usually quick to respond to community enquiries, but a worrying number seem to hide who they are in a complex web of company names and post office box addresses.

The policy and politics of fair access to land – and the open source and low cost data to track land – needs to be part of the grant making programme for placemaking. Land advocacy in all its guises is a king pin for community placemaking, autonomy and the development of social, economic and environment area-based assets.

5. disruptive grant making: via placemaking

the *place* making factor:

Advocacy and Cities Film Fest Poster, New York

creating placemaking disruption

"Grant makers seem to be hooked to the traditional...their reticent towards understanding social and environmental connections, and that's frustrating they need to think outside their usual boxes."

Grant making or funding from charitable foundations for a placemaking strategy , makes for a fairer society, and a more precise way of supporting communities disenfranchised from the current grant making in England. Sure, it will mean disrupting the way foundations think and talk about not just the environment or people but placemaking, and how they fund it.

"Placemaking has disruptive potential. The ability to stop siloed working. It should focus on issues governance scales and management that can facilitate place capital."

The grant makers I spoke to in the US and the UK showed an interest in placemaking. What struck me most is that the US, especially in cities like New York, Detroit, Pittsburgh, and Philadelphia understood the place factor, and its power to fund environment and people as part of systems change. And at the heart of that change is using placemaking, as a convergence model for grant makers and charitable foundations, or philanthropists to provide donations, grants, and capital investment.

grant funding types

In the US, the grant funding of placemaking ranges from small scale to large and cross-sector collaborative:

small to medium scale charitable foundation grant funding: small endowments from individuals and small to large foundations, e.g. Kresge Foundation providing $42,000 to CDAD to act as a local placemaking grant maker funding to small or tactical short-term projects.

medium to large scale charitable foundation grant funding: here the role of placemaking is attached to a wider set of contexts such as poverty, jobs or community resilience, e.g. the Knights Foundation $5 Million City Challenge, the Ford Foundation's Metropolitan Opportunities Programme, and the Kresge Foundation use major placemaking projects and strategies as a means of, tackling urban renewal and inequality agendas.

private sector to social sector grant funding, and collaborative partnerships with social sector organisations: For example, PPS (Projects for Public Space) a not-for -profit organisation and Southwest Airlines – where PPS provides grants to cities connected to the Airline, from 50k to $100k average, 6 per year)

What's interesting is that any one of these forms of grant funding interprets placemaking as a catalyst for areas of social and economic change:

- civil/political: advocacy, litigation and reform

- analytical: research, policy analysis, data collation
- capacity and skills building: training, volunteering, accelerating job opportunities, local economy investment
- collaboration: supporting cross and inter-sector collaboration
- discussion: strategic, coordinated co-creation between charities' different programmes and/or with other charitable foundations or private sector initiatives specifically as part of an inclusive urban agenda

factor six

If placemaking is to be a disrupter, there are six factors that grant makers need to be clear on:

1. place led not place based

What's essential for all grant funders, not just environment grant makers is to remember that placemaking is a Place Led model. Not a Place Based model.

So to be clear, grant funding for place and placemaking is really not the same as place based grant funding. The latter focuses on geographical or city based grants, where grant makers concentrate on getting grants into 'coldspot' areas. The geographic areas they have not previously adequately funded, or where their remit is to provide a grant to a particular area or areas.

"the starting point is to lead with the common interest in a place, then to create spaces where people, can learn together, validate and share common interest

2. place is political

The thing with placemaking is that it probably sounds to some a bit fluffy, somehow akin to cupcake baking. But it isn't.

Sorry. Property for sale, East London

Greenwich Village, New York

Placemaking is sometimes interpreted as a 'soft sell' – this is reflected by an interviewee who said, "dreadful developers use it as a term to just make a place look pretty. It's all about selling their houses for a higher price.

Research shows that the physical results of good placemaking can increase house prices, and build local economies. It also shows that it can address the kind of gentrification that prices people with low incomes out of a place to live. But, research reveals that placemaking can also increase wellbeing, create jobs and improve co-creation. That's something I know progressive developers and grant funders alike want to be part of.

Placemaking is an alternative response to the traditional notion of place being owned only by the affluent. Most advocates and practitioners of placemaking, question the legitimacy of such ownership. The challenge thrown into the ring is whether placemaking is solely abou t legal ownership by the few. At the heart of placemaking is the fundamental belief that places are for all, and not only for profit.

It means philanthropists or organisations that grant fund placemaking will have to confront significant issues: a rolled backed state, and the passing on of public spaces and places to communities. There's an urgent need to develop new models of ownership and use, not only for parks and green spaces but grey space and buildings too, if they are to survive austerity, local authority cuts and land banking. But Janette Sadik-Khan, the former New York Commissioner for the Department of Transportation, noted for her role in implementing New York's placemaking agenda, was right when she said:

> *"Saying no to new developments is not enough –*
> *we need agendas cities can say yes to."*

As people increasingly get involved in the making of places we need any kind of reform to be reflective and accountable. Joseph Stiglitz, Nobel Peace Prize economist and author of The Great Divide, suggests this is how democracy is changed to restore prosperity for all.

3. lead and ask 'difficult' questions

When I'm discussing placemaking with grant makers in the US and the UK, there is a sense of dissatisfaction with the current conversation around the environment. In the last eighteen months, I've seen a step change – from people asking what placemaking is to government departments, quangos and communities recognising that placemaking is a potential game changer. But their primary concern is that the current debate on grant making is failing to factor in placemaking as a catalyst to disrupt social and environmental grant making.

Grant makers massively shape social change, so there's an obligation on them to lead on placemaking. They need to step-up and invest in placemaking, share the learning, the fails and the wins, and ask challenging questions about the social and inclusion benefits of a project. It's not enough to accept slick grant proposals from large NGOs who can quote multiple index deprivation figures of the areas they're working in, without asking, 'Exactly how is the project going to work with the deprived communities? How is it going to create training and jobs? Will the project develop community business? And just how does the project fully support and partner with diverse and excluded communities? ' These are particularly salient questions when investing in placemaking, for those who need it most, and not only hipster projects that can aggravate adverse impacts of gentrification.

'this is about developing paradigm changes that move from the usual and the ordinary to the extraoordinary'

4. share the learning and the data

In conversations with charitable organisations, I often hear how the staff are keen to learn more about place and about implementing the place factor. But, there's always a point where they worry about how to 'sell it' to their Board, most notably, the Boards of trustees who have a personal connection to traditional environmental conservation or poverty alleviation grant funding – though some have mentioned that there are one or two particularly younger Board members who 'get it'.

'The first generation was about conservation ...the third generation is more interested in people as part of the habitat. They see environment through a social justice lens...their view is more about the urban: parks, gardens, river fronts, and creating spaces for better living, and develop thinking on how that happens'.

Board. Introduce them to members of other Boards who are interested in place; provide them with the information they need to champion place at Board level and get other Board members hooked.

The candid response of one senior member of a grant foundation was clear about the need to appeal to the Board's ego by illustrating how using the place factor can develop the foundation's leadership role in the sector.

Let's be clear about this: though the change at Board level won't happen overnight, grant making foundations have to be thinking of ways to provide that impetus – over, and over again until it sticks.

Like the US Place Making Funders' Forum, the UK also needs a Forum of Place Making Funders. In the US, the Forum is a collaboration of Foundations, businesses, the social sector and commercial worlds, where data informs decisions, tricky problems are outed, and there's learning from both wins and failures, and most importantly, making the case for environmental and social inclusion through placemaking.

Grant funding placemaking creates more chances for impact and engages more communities and individual as change makers. It's fertile ground for data collection and learning, not only for grant makers, but also the wider public.

"We are now living in a data driven world, where data needs to be democratically available to everyone ."

Data needs to define the place factor: it should look at the level of grants, the type of funder, the geographical location, the community and it demographics (including income levels, education attainment, age, ethnicity, etc.) to see just where the funding holes are.

"Data collection is crucial for understanding where grant making is going in real time. We are tracking primary and secondary grant making. It's data that will show [us] some of the deep dive learning we need."

While organisations like the Environmental Funders Network in England, the Environmental Grantmakers Network, and the Environment and Health Network in the US are collating data, the difficult thing is how to assess or use the data to trace the 'how, why, when and where' of grant funding place and green spaces. In England, this data gap leaves the sector with a less than helpful data vacuum on placemaking. Capitalising on the placemaking factor requires accessible quantitative and qualitative research.

5. fund for longer, fund core and fund fair

It's been said. Many times before. But it needs to be said again: three years' grant funding is just not enough.

"What we have to do is long term investment for local people and social enterprises that could become big and impactful before and beyond three.years."

Grant makers in the US and the UK have shown an understanding that this type of grant funding is short term and rarely helps to cement the successful projects beyond the point of a test bed or pilot project. Many place projects need up to ten years' grant support. They are more often up against turning around decades of decay, and sometimes demoralised, fractious communities who may well be collaborating for the first time, and to top it off the wrong type of private investor where profit is the only motivator.

While the localism agenda and the Localism Act (2011) offers neighbourhoods in England and Wales the potential to manage and own assets, the Act has potential an incredibly useful tool for community led placemaking, co-ownership and community asset building. But I see too many communities struggling with these new asset rights. And that's because the rolling back of the state also means that environmental assets and duties of care for them are sometimes passed on to communities without the required resources, skills and budgets to create successful long-term projects. The long-term commitment of ten-year grants or endowments like that of England's Big Lottery to projects such as The Local Trust or potentially Power for Change needs to be the norm.

A tenet of placemaking is that 'creating better places is not about the money'. I'd like to push back on this. Money is a crucial resource for levering training and creating jobs with living wages. While thousands of people provide volunteer time in green spaces, environmental and local economy projects, working for free is not a choice everyone can or wants to make. For everyone to be able to bring their skills, experience and ideas to the table, there needs to be an option for fair remuneration.

For the placemaking factor to work, this is crucial.

6. don't always go solo – collaborate

"Unfortunately collaboration is not the usual starting point.. the predominate model of operation is that each foundation has boards and staff that just wish the others would follow their cause because theirs is the right one"

Austerity cuts are already having an impact on public sector funding. Local authorities are reporting worryingly significant percentage cuts in planning, and community and environmental services. So public sector funding can't be relied on to fund placemaking. But the exciting thing about the placemaking factor is that it offers a brilliant model for collaboration and co-creation.

"...it's time to invest in long lasting change through collaboration and ownership with multiple stakeholders on all aspects of placemaking."

Diagrams 1 and 2 earlier in the book illustrate the social, economic and political connectors that allow alignment across different grant funder remits.

Opening up grant foundation doors to placemaking sparks community action, environmental stewardship, local economies and wellbeing. In doing so, small- to large-scale funders, philanthropists and businesses wanting to invest in and support community development, social enterprises and land management should be funding small- and large- scale projects together, bringing the resources but also the data skills and experience that tripartite projects need to harness social, private and public sector.

6.
finally

In any movement for change, investors (monetary and non-monetary) and grant making foundations are imperative for investing in the placemaking agenda And, the placemaking factor provides the most perfect of opportunities to do just that.

Disruption can, by its nature, be unsettling – it's about change and upheaval – but it's also about growth and progress. People and the places or spaces, they live, work, love and play in deserve that.

acknowledgements

Thanks to:

The Esmée Fairbairn Foundation: Jenny Dadd, Sharon Shea, Caroline Mason and John Mulligan for their support.

The Clore Social Leadership Programme team, Dame Mary Marsh , Liz Lowther and Louise Hooper.

The the many individuals who not only gave their time, knowledge, and experience, but were willing to offer candid reflections. They include Ed Anderton, Vanessa E Bonnelly, Caroline Broadhurst, Ethan Kent, Fred Kent, Jane McIntosh, Barbra Mazur, Justin G Moore, Penny Fujiko Willgerodt, Peter Scollard, Paula Z Segal and Kathy Session.

My family Christoph, Ellena and Edward, Victor, and Tayo. My friends and colleagues, in particular, Emma Herbert, for their consistent encouragement, and my fellow writing partners in crime, Baljeet Sandhu, Louise Canon and Sanjeev Lingayah.

And, last but definitely not least, to my mother Grace Olurin-Adebowale, who taught me that everyone has a right to a decent livelihood, a healthy environment and a good place to live; but also a responsibility to each other to make sure that happens.

maria adebowale-schwarte www.mariaadebowale.com

references

Carl Adams, Northfleet Big Local, http://northfleetbiglocal.com (Accessed 12th August 2015)

Maria Adebowale, Urban Deprivation and the Built Environment, Prospect Magazine http://wwwprospect magazine.co.uk/wp-content/uploads/2013/11/jrf_web.pdf, (2015)

Aldo van Eyck, (quoted from) Aldo Van Eyck and the city as [a] playground, Merijn Oudenampsen https://merijnoudenampsen.org/2013/03/27/aldo-van-eyck-and-the-city-as-playground/ (Accessed June 2016)

CDAD, http://cdad-online.org/placemaking/ (Accessed 1st August, 2015)

Department of Community and Local Government, 'A Plain English Guide to the Localism Act, https://www.gov.uk/government/uploads/system/uploads/attachement_data/file/5959/1896534.pdf (2011)

Five Nine Six Acres, http://596acres.org (Accessed 1st August, 2015) Ford Foundation, https://www.fordfoundation.org (Accessed 20th June 2015)

Green Space definition, Google definitionhttps://www.google.co.uk/search?client=safari&rls=en&q=green+space+definition&ie=UTF - 8&oe=UTF-8&gfe_rd=cr&ei=CpVNV-vkEIye7AbH8JiIDA# (Accessed 28th Sept 2015)

Greening Detroit, http://www.greeningofdetroit.com (Accessed 20th June 2015)

Goal 11, United Nations Sustainable Development Goals http://www.un.org/sustainabledevelopment/cities/ (Accessed 1st June 2016)

Tim Heath, Professor Taner Oc, and Steve Tiesdell, pg 122, Public Places Urban Spaces, The Dimensions of Urban Design, 2nd Edition, Edited by Matthew Carmona, Routledge Press (2013)

ICLEI (Informed Cities), Rotterdam, Which way to the future? Strategies, tools and inspiration for transforming cities, http://informed-cities.iclei-europe.org/index.php?id=8524 (Accessed Nov 13th 2015)

Jane Jacobs, pg 83, The Death and Life of Great American Cities, The Modern Library (1993)

Knights Foundation, http://www.knightfoundation.org/articles/5-million-knight-cities-challenge-opens-oct-10 (Accessed October 2nd 2016)

Kresge Foundation, http://kresge.org (Accessed July 22nd 2015)

Lafayette Greens Garden - Detroit, You Tube, https://www.youtube.com/watch?v=GGTye8Ifjk4 (Accessed January 5th 2016) 3

Living Space Project, http://livingspaceproject.com/projects (Accessed 12th August 2015)

Localism Act 2011, http://www.legislation.gov.uk/ukpga/2011/20/contents/enacted (Accessed 12th June 2016)

Local Trust, http://localtrust.org.uk (Accessed 12th August 2015)

No Wall Gardens film: People, Place and Environment, http://livingspaceproject.com/our-projects/ (Accessed 12th August 2015)

PPS (Projects for Public Spaces), South West Airlines heart of the community, http://www.pps.org/heart-of-the-community/ (Accessed 10th October 2015)

Richard Rogers, Cities for a Small Planet, pg 4, Faber & Faber (1997)

Janet Sadik-Khan & Seth Solomonow, What Would Jane Jacobs Do: Why the question remains so vital today, City Lab, http://www.citylab.com/design/2016/05/why-we-ask-ourselves-what-would-jane-jacobs-do/481422/ (Accessed 5th May 2016)

Joseph E. Stiglitz, The Great Divide, Penguin (2015)

Erik Swyngedouw and Nikolas C. Heynen, Urban Political Ecology, Justice and the Politics of Scale, Chapter 8, (pg 80), The Blackwell City Reader, 2nd Edition, Edited Gary Bridge & Sophie Dickson, Wiley & Blackwell (2010)

images

all photos and images are by the author unless otherwise stated

the author

Placemaking and urban renewal strategist, Maria Adebowale-Schwarte specialises in place led prosperity, green spaces, cross-sector collaboration, and community participation.

She's the Founding Director of Living Space Project, an urban placemaking think tank and consultancy that works with charitable foundations, government, the social sector, communities, developers and urban place makers in the public and private sectors. Maria is also an advisor to grant makers on environment and placemaking.

Her background is in planning and environment law and she holds a Masters in Law, from the University of London. She is on a number of executive board and committees of placemaking, environment, and heritage organisations. In addition, Maria is a member of the International Place Making Council, an affiliate member of the Royal Institute of British Architects, and the first recipient of the Clore Social Leadership Environment Fellowship. She also sits on number of boards and committees of organisations with place led and environment agendas.

She has written for The Guardian, Prospect Magazine, New Start Magazine, the Organisation for Economic Cooperation and Development, The Town and Country Planning Journal, the World Bank, the Joseph Rowntree Foundation, the British Academy and Policy Press.

notes:

notes:

notes:

27881369R00042

Printed in Great Britain
by Amazon